MIND PASTRY
by the 2022 CLIL Senior Year

Loi n°49-956 du 16 juillet 1949 sur les publications destinées à la jeunesse, modifiée par la loi n°2011-525 du 17 mai 2011.

© 2022, A02 class
Édition : BoD – Books on Demand, info@bod.fr
Impression : BoD – Books on Demand,
In de Tarpen 42, Norderstedt (Allemagne)
Impression à la demande
ISBN : 978-2-3223-9250-6
Dépôt légal : Juin 2022

Inside his mind…

Even after all we have endured and all we have lived, I am still able to utter those words: "You're the ray of light which enhances every moment of my life." I know I'm no longer the man of your life, since our divorce; everything has changed. However, I still have in my heart and soul, memories of your cherry lipstick that you knew I love, the dress that you wore for our first date that wine had stained. I also remember the littlest aspect of your routine: the orange juice you'd like right after waking up, the religious way you never finished any single cup of tea, the way you danced after dinner…

    I now can understand why people commonly say "we're breaking up", that's because they are conscientiously tearing themselves apart, flagellating every remembrance, echo of their late loved ones. Anyway, even if I can now acknowledge some functions that way, I would never feel it in my deep being. Why? You're seriously asking me why? Because Ariadne. Because it was you and it was me as a poet once said. Because you are a part of me, embedded in my flesh. Because no matter what, you taught me how to live in full consciousness and not only to be satisfied with surviving with the only need that is called necessity.

Even if we divorced, I will always love and cherish you. I promise. You were my best friend. You are still my best friend, Ariadne.

By Axelle Carpentier,
Winner of the Speakeasy Creative Writing Competition - C1

TRAVEL

My wonderful New Year … or not

This morning, I was so glad to make my brother discover Chinese New Year. Animation, food… everything was so exciting!

Blinded by the excitement of the surrounding events, I exclaimed:

"Come on, take a look at this shirt!"

Since he didn't answer me, I turned around but he wasn't there anymore! Starting to panic, I began to observe the surroundings. The noises that seemed so welcoming to me were now just a deafening noise.

Instinctively and subconsciously, I ran towards an alley lit in red, the fault of the lanterns which were arranged there. But no one was there…

Disoriented by the frantic beating of my heart, I veered sharply to the right down a very dark street. I was afraid that my brother could be there… The pressure was overwhelming now and my entire members were shaking.

What if something had happened to him?

My legs, which hadn't stopped moving, led me to a large avenue where a big parade was taking place.

23h59

I no longer counted the minutes. Was it raining or was I crying? I had lost all hope…

00h00

And that's when he appeared under the sky lit up with colorful fireworks… Blowing all the air out of my lungs, I whispered.

"Thanks God everything is fine now"

Yaël Pecqueux

Sound of waves

It was a summer afternoon. I had gone on vacation without my parents for the first time and with my friend squad. We decided to go to St Tropez. We were all happy in the sun to enjoy the beach, to get up early in the morning to go to the market, stroll among the olive trees and picnic in the lavender fields. That day we went to the beach to spend an afternoon enjoying the sea and the sun kissing our skin. The sound of the waves calming us, the children laughing made us smile, the catchy summer music blackmailed us all; the holidays, the loud laughter of my friends made me discover happiness. I loved that part of me able to discover every moment of happiness away from everything. That day our friendship was even stronger and we knew this vacation was going to be one of our best memories. I often think about this afternoon at the beach, it makes me remember how beautiful life is and how much I miss my friends.

Vivi

It was a special day. My friend and I had just taken one last picture of our vacation in Australia. These vacations taught me a lot about team cohesion and training, indeed we had planned to go to this place and it was the best decision of our summer.

On the 4th of July 2021, my friends just told me to leave France for a three weeks' trip.

My close friend from high school, Angele, had proposed to buy our plane tickets, with my three other friends, at the airport of Paris.

We had wanted to go on a trip together for so long and our dream finally came true this summer.

The 24 hours' flight went too fast, we didn't even realize we were on the other side of the earth.

Moreover, during the second week, we were sleeping in an Airbnb that we had rented for the whole stay.

One evening, after a nice time in a lovely restaurant, on the way home my friend remembered that he had forgotten the keys to the apartment in the rental.

We had to call a locksmith and our deposit was not returned unfortunately…

Despite this unfortunate event, which now makes us laugh, our holidays have enriched us for the rest of our lives.

I hope you have already had the chance to leave with loved ones and if that is not the case, I dare you!

Moreau Emma

We met ten years ago and I remember it as if it was yesterday… We met back in sixth grade, we were so young and so shy, but time being together made us grow up. This meeting is unforgettable, when I think about it I have chills and I will do everything to go back once again. And if I didn't know her, how would my life be? This girl quickly became a confidante, she knew all my little secrets, all my health problems and also my anxiety. I considered her my soulmate, we had the same inside jokes, the same thoughts, the same ideas… In those 10 years we've been through a lot, both good and bad, where we've always been there for each other. Indeed, thanks to her words and her smile, my sadness began to fade away, she was always there for me as I was always there for her. We spent every week together, glued together, our evenings were all about eating pizza, karaoke, dancing, laughing about our childhood memories. Unfortunately all good things come to an end, my best friend had to go away from here, away from me for her professional project. I can't be selfish and I have to think about her well so I let her go despite my heart still bleeding… Her departure was a month ago, and it still hurts me today. I remember the rainy weather of this Thursday, February 12th, her unique and faithful perfume that she has had for 15 years, her silver jewelry that she admired so much, and then finally her pretty shirt that she wore at every great occasion. I don't think you can imagine the excruciating pain of seeing one's best friend, one's confidante, one's half go away. She had become my everything. I find myself alone today. How can I do without her? Without her my life means nothing, my minutes have become hours, my seconds minutes. I hope to find her again someday, she'll find me. Then I hope for you to find a friend like mine, someone who can listen to you, advise you, console you, make you laugh and make you think of something else when everything goes wrong. She's a sister God didn't give me…

H.C

My inner child

She was a dreamer and she grew up admiring Rihanna, Shakira, Beyonce, Olivia Ruiz, and other powerful female singers. She used to tuck her belly in, because these singers had a flat stomach. It was said pretty girls were skinny.
When winter was coming, she believed Santa Claus would come offer her Barbie dolls, princess dresses. She used to have fun in the snow, but also fun in the sand and in the grass. All she wanted was to feel like this forever. But also she was little, and she was confused that adults didn't listen to her enough.
Life through her eyes was amazing, unreal. Everything was colors and music. How curious she was about this new world. How free she felt, how little she felt compared to everything.
She used to sing a lot, yell a lot, dance a lot. She expected the world.
She grew up learning about love, and boys, and how she wanted to be noticed by them. How it's important to be pretty to be interesting. All they did to her was harm. She cried often when her heart felt too big for her body and when her brain couldn't understand. All she wanted was to live in her fantasy. But other kids couldn't understand her. Her heart was so pure but so breakable.

She wanted to become a ballerina, a singer, a stylist, a rock star, a superhero. But every time reality hit her dreams felt more and more distant.

She used to spend the summers in her grandparents' countryside house. There her best memories are built. This house is now on sale since her grandpa passed away. Where did she go? She seems so gone now. It's like she's fading away as years fly by.

Life was easy when everything wasn't so real, so sad, so harsh. Her parents did their best to protect their little girl from the world, but every time she left home she was exposed. How could those little boys touch her? Insult her? Why are they now happier than her?

She was so aware of her body too early, and how other people see it.

She was just a little girl. I lost her.

Lila

FRIENDSHIP

C&D

Lying peacefully under the summer sunlight, the two friends were contemplating their lives. Little did they know all the adventures they would live and all the lands they would explore when they became friends five decades ago. Needless to say this friendship was not meant to be; never had Deedee ever seen such an abrasive goat!

They used to graze in the same meadow, where a variety of marvelous flowers could be found. This landscape was a sight for sore eyes, and it made Deedee take the decision to try and befriend this unknown goat, whom she'd later know the name was Chouchou. She approached her at a snail's pace lest she got scared. When Deedee found herself at a fair distance of Chouchou, she asked slowly:

"Hi, I'm Deedee and I thought we could become friends, since we both often hang out around here. What's your name?"

Chouchou glanced at Deedee. Wow, if looks could kill…

"Who said I'd like to be friends with you?" Chouchou replied harshly. "Leave me alone you dirty goat." she added, before turning her back on Deedee.

"How dare she give me the cold shoulder! Well, she can go to hell for all I care!"

The following days, Deedee made sure not to run into Chouchou, and she was determined not to cross her path again!

Destiny had other plans for them though; they were forced to go through ordeals and hardships during a grueling quest that'd be too long for me to tell you.

Well, they seem to think that life is just a bowl of cherries right now; maybe we can go and ask them to tell us more of their story?

N. A

It was on a random Tuesday. Not a Tuesday like the others. It was the Tuesday we met again after 10 years... Here on this bench I was waiting for them to come. I could hear the birds chirping, the kids playing on the playground...remembering that it was once us. I was sitting here as alone as I had been for the past few years.

I didn't know what to do and how to act.

What would they look like now? What job would they do? Had they thought about me during this time? I just had so many questions...

As time passed by I looked back on our moments that we had spent together that I cherished a lot and thought about how much they meant to me.

The closer they'd get to me, the more sparkles would erupt in my stomach.

Suddenly I felt that someone was coming closer to me, I lifted my eyes and could see their long blond hair, their wide blue eyes pointing at me and it was at this time that the fireworks inside me exploded.

I felt like I had started living again for the first time in ten years. The person I spent all of my childhood with, my partner in crime, my soulmate... My best friend was back into my life.

I got up a bit awkwardly without knowing how to greet them, should I just hug them, shake their hands? Yet, it went really naturally just like it was before. I missed everything about them even small details that could only be theirs, such as their smell, their hair color and how bright their smile was.

We started talking and I noticed that I could still be my true self when I was around them; I was not scared of laughing out loud in front of everyone else nor to confess myself about what had happened in my life all those wasted years. Nothing around me mattered except for them, I could have listened to their voice for hours, I wouldn't have complained.

Since that afternoon, I pray every single day for this gem of human being to stay in my life. I need them by my side all life long and I'll do anything for it. We may have lost ten years but we have our entire life to live together now.

Emma C.

     The guy next to me in the photograph is probably the most important friend in my life.
We messed around whenever possible. I had a million adventures with him and that gave me so many memories. I feel really nostalgic talking about this.
The photograph was taken the last night I saw him. I remember it as if it was yesterday. It's Théo,
I've known him for more than 16 years and he supported me in good and bad times.
He was a year older so he could give me a lot of advice. I remember that it was the day before that night that he announced his moving to the South of France. So we both knew this would be our last day together.
   The 4th of July 2010, for our last day, we decided to spend the day at the beach, eating ice cream and drinking lemonade. We said everything we had never told each other, all deep secrets inside us. At the end of the day, some friends joined us and we were all able to swim together in the still warm sea of the afternoon. In the evening we both returned by bike, it was as if time had stopped.
     We were two carefree young people, happy to be there, together, in the night.

E. G

I & THEM

The story of an old woman who dwells in Montmartre in Paris.

She lives alone in her luxurious flat. She watches everyone from her window; anyone who walks into this alley will be seen by this lady. Whoever you are, a child, an adult, a teenager or an old man, she analyses you. Indeed that dame reads in you, imagines your life and finally understands you. She knows if you are sad, happy, nervous, tired… She loves to see young people because it gives her a youthful feeling.

In the 80's she was 17 years old she was a mysterious and beautiful girl. She met a handsome boy. They fell in love and lived their best life for ten years. The two lovebirds lived the perfect relationship in the city of love with stars in their eyes. They grew up together, traveled a lot around the world and discovered real life, the good and the bad nevertheless they had always overcome everything together. Until the day when her beloved caught cancer and died…

This event broke her heart and her whole soul. She never got over it. Not a day goes by without her thinking about him.

That's why now this old lady lives through bystanders.

Eug

"We were in the '80s when the Korean civil war started. You see, kids, it was at that time your Dad and I met, it was in that same classroom you can see in this picture. "This is the classroom we hid in in 1987, it was the year when one of the biggest and savage demonstrations took place …" At that time your Dad and I were college students, he was just a year older than me. He had just come back from a semester abroad and I was failing my classes as usual. But you already know this. Now let's go back to our story; so where was I, oh yes, the demonstration of Busan: as I said it was the worst ever seen, and as the big coward I was, I decided to go and hide in an apparently abandoned middle school. I tried to open the main gate and it was surprisingly open… This should have made me think twice before entering it, I was completely dumb when I was in college if you want my opinion.

I entered the building with a weird feeling; most of the lights were flickering, which increased the awkward atmosphere. I, to be honest, wasn't very adventurous, so I entered the first classroom that was open, it was classroom 101, it was the second door on the left when you entered the building. The room was in complete silence and the only source of light was a street lamp, so the lighting was very poor, that is why I didn't see your dad at first glance. So I entered the room and out of nowhere I started crying, I was really terrified at the time. This is when I saw him for the first time, in the corner of the classroom, he seemed nearly as terrified as I was, so I went to meet him to perhaps present myself to him. I honestly just went to see him, and to feel less alone crying… he was not. We started talking to each other .I was a little forcing him to talk since he didn't want to… yet I did make him talk to me, so we started to discuss our lives and somehow the feeling was passing pretty good, to a point that we talked until the next day. Thanks to him I forgot about the horrible demonstration, I spent one of the best nights I had ever had. Since that day we have never separated from each other. And this, my kids, is how I met your dad. See, sometimes horrible things can lead you to a long life relationship."

Martin.L

THE FIRST TO SUCCOMB.

The mystic mesmerizing being
That is the mermaid in my glance
Tantalizes and attracts my skin
Towards an enticing depth.

Yet in another world
Where the roles would be switched
You would be seen as a core
Of a consuming heat.

She would spy on you from afar
Like a mirage that in a hope of living
Would see in you a way of loving

Her gaze and yours complementing each other
With this wall of water as a border
Who would be the first...

M E

FROM DREAM TO NIGHTMARE

This picture was taken in the summer 2020; it was a very sunny and funny afternoon.
First we met up with some friends to chill out at the beach then we felt a wind breeze in our hair and that's the moment when we knew it was time to go kite surfing.
We put on our wetsuits and we were gone for a long ride. Nevertheless that time would be very special as a seal was following us and one of my friends was absolutely terrified about it!
He kept saying: « It will bite me! » and couldn't stop crying. We were all laughing at him when suddenly we couldn't see him any longer and that's also when we started to panic too so we returned to the beach to seek for help. The rescue services were quickly activated for his search and there was even a helicopter. A thick fog rose, we could not see anything! However despite the fog we did not let go to save our friend. We were on the verge of giving up when the emergency services claimed to have found him. The gourmet he was had simply gone to get a waffle without telling us. Everything went back to normal after we were chastised.
 I must say I'm not about to forget that afternoon.

J. J

Akuna Matata

In the ancient farm I used to live in, life was exhausting. It was such an intensively animated place, I couldn't lower my guard a single second, at any time a squad of mice could appear behind me and chase me through the whole building. What a harsh life for a kitty! At the top of my prickly straw bales tower, admiring the countryside landscape, I was wondering: "Had another life been possible, where food would have popped up in front of me every morning… It would have been heaven on earth…".

Suddenly I heard a distant roar coming towards me. A woman came out of a car and visited the place. A cascade of questions came to my mind. What was she looking for? Only one way to find out: I had to follow her. As an experienced spy, I sneaked behind her. Nevertheless, my nature as a cat got the better of me and an inescapable low "meow" went out of my mouth marking a watershed in my life. She picked me up and noticed I was alone here, as a consequence she decided to bring me to her place.

I woke up in such a comfortable warm bed, surrounded by two children who just wanted to cuddle me. The best thing was that a large bowl full of delicious treats had been put next to me! From this day on, my life became a dream: I did not have to run and hunt anymore, everything was given to me every time I mewed! Akuna Matata, what a gorgeous life for a kitty!

DELLYS Quentin

Others.

Eyes. A lot of eyes. All eyes on me. One by one, they appear and disappear. They're looking at me. They're looking for me. Waiting for me to make one mistake. Scrutinizing for when I lose my balance and appreciating my falls, always. They are screaming in my head. Screaming harsh and incomprehensible words without interruptions. Invading my brain, exploding my forefront. « It's all in my head », people said. But I can see them, hear them, sense them, feel them: all pointing at me. Their long and twisted fingers approaching my head, warping my face by grappling my cheeks. Tearing my hair out, scratching my eyes, pulling my teeth out. I can't scream, they have just cut my tongue. Only a gravelly rale could escape from my blue throat. That blood, that tear, that sweat: fear. The only way I can exist. Why? I couldn't support it any longer, I let them do anything to me. My body belonged to them. My heart was kept cloistered in their silly hands. What have you done to me? What did I become? What Am I? A childish play, the aim; shaping my soul, forming my Being. Build and rebuild. Create or Destroy. Recognize me as you want me to be. Nobody cares whether or not I exist. Nothing has changed. I pretended not to see it at first. Yet here is the evidence I must accept.

Say something! Convince me that you care about me! Lie to me! Tell me what I need to hear to return to my comfortable denial again!
Choose my seat! Choose my choices! Choose my Me! Choose everything it needs for you to love me. I'm begging you! Don't kill me! Don't leave me alone! I don't want to be alone.

Those eyes…

Axelle Carpentier

A nightmare

« Come on kids, it's time to go »
With these words John opened the door, put his skis on his shoulders and walked out.
It had been four days since the family arrived in the mountains, John skied with his children as his wife was unfortunately injured on the first day
Paul and William were two fifteen year old twins, passionate about snow sports, strong feelings and always ready to follow their father in these adventures

Today the weather was beautiful, and it was the famous off-piste day

It was barely nine o'clock, John, Paul and William were already down the slopes, ready to take the chair lift.

They had prepared very well, their backpacks full of GPS, detectors and phones. The day looked excellent

The off-piste was almost a religion there, once at the top of the slopes, it was then necessary to walk to the top of the mountain for nearly two hours.

Once at the top, the view over the whole valley was magnificent

But no time to lose, John went first and it was a great sight for the eyes.

His silhouette undulated between the rocks and the trees; he arrived at the bottom in time to film his children descending at the same time.

Paul and William went for it, the snow was good and the twins skied beautifully.

Suddenly, with a crashing noise, a whole section of the mountain seemed to come off.

An avalanche took place, in front of John's helpless eyes.

With a deafening noise, John immediately lost sight of his sons...

After a few minutes that seemed like an eternity, William, out of breath, completely frozen and with tears on his cheeks, found his father.

However, Paul was nowhere to be found, and the sun was about to set.

Time was running out and John decided to call the police.

Helicopters and dogs came and went but no trace of Paul was found.

Paul was alive but stuck under a layer of snow and his hours were numbered.

It was finally John himself who found his son, at nightfall, by digging behind a rock.

Paul, William and John were all together at the bottom, surrounded by the police, looking for an explanation after this huge scare

John spoke up and...

Driiiiiiiiiiiiing

"Come on kids, it's nine o'clock and time to go skiing »

Antoine

Waterfall

It occurred on a bright, sunny Sunday of July in the south. The atmosphere was more than pure and the landscape conveyed a deep feeling in everybody's heart. Lots of people used to come and go to see this astonishing marvel, nonetheless it has been three days since anyone last came. Don't you think this is the perfect place to do something peculiar?

It all started when a family of two parents and two children from the north of the country came here, far from their natural habitat. They had been eager to go on vacation for a whole year; the sun, the rivers, the mountains and so on. The family did a trip that lasted twelve hours in a tiny city car, with all the luggage in its boot which made it even heavier and thus, less powerful to escape from something.
They laid down their hat with a feeling of completeness combined with the cloudless, deep blue sky reflecting on their skin. Albeit they were exhausted from sitting at the back of a soapbox racer, they immediately began to empty

their suitcases so as to feel at home. Though, they did not settle in a huge mansion but in a remote kind of shack in the middle of a grape field with a pool. This pool was located down the path when they wanted to go out to the river that was five minutes away. After a couple of days the family decided to leave for going to an astounding location, again they had to use that same car for moving there. The same car, the same number of people, the same luggage.

That's it, after half an hour of travel they made it to the waterfall. They expected a huge quantity of people, nevertheless it was on a Sunday.

They were not really on the lookout for odd events and yet, they should have been. As they went deeper into the forest, the only thing they could hear was water, dripping and streaming from nowhere.

They reached the summit of the waterfall, grazing the top of the trees where they could catch a glimpse of the marvelous panorama.

Yet suddenly there was another noise, loud and shrill, coming from where they entered the site.

They thought it was time to leave. The descent was harder than the climb obviously, however the path was not similar to what they had seen the first time. Footprints could be distinguished, but not only theirs. They were walking faster and faster.

They reached the car. But it did not start, as the noises were getting closer.

Livio. M

DEATH

That sweet summer night

And now let's listen to our reporter live, amidst numerous bombings and screams during the war in…». I turn the radio off, knowing that the news will, as always, be atrocious.

It is 10:30 p.m and I'm still furrowing the empty streets of my city, heading to the petrol station. I'm convinced my mom would be so mad at me for leaving work that late, but it was a turmoil day and I was determined to finish my work in hand. I'll just keep it as a secret between you and me.

As I'm getting out of my car, a ghastly thud coupled with a weird flash startled me while sending shivers down my spine. What is this? I lift my head to catch a glimpse of the place where the sound came from.

And I see it.
It is huge.
And I also hear screams.
They are dreadful.

This is the moment when I understood. It was the end for me. No need to run away nor to yell. A gigantic oblong warhead is falling down right above my head.

This is the moment when I understood that I only had 20 seconds left to live.

20

Breathing gets harder and harder as a vise tightens around my chest. My whole body is shaking and tears are now rolling down my cheeks.

Should I call my family, my friends? No I don't have enough time.

I can't imagine how dreadful it will be for them to hear the news on TV. They will go through so much pain because of me.

I'm so sorry.

15

How can human create such a terrible object? War is such an absurd event: inviting anonymous people to kill each other for no personal reason. I will die for a country that will not even remember me.

What is sure is that this day is closing this old debate between Hobbes and Rousseau. Hobbes was right, mankind is evil. That's it.

10

I was supposed to call my parents tonight, narrating my exhausting day.

I was supposed to offer that cute plush to my brother when coming back home.
I was supposed to obtain my diploma.
I was supposed to celebrate it with my besties.
I was supposed to get the job of my dream.
I was supposed to meet the right person.
I was supposed to fall in love.
I was supposed to start a family.
I was supposed to adopt a dog.
I was supposed to become a grandma.
I was supposed to, one day, die of old age.

But before that, I was supposed to live.

5

The sky is clear and millions of stars are watching the same spectacle as me, as us. A turquoise trail detaches from the bomb, misplacing countless bronze particles on its way.

4

How can such a contrast coexist in the same sweet summer night?

3

I hope the most precious people to me…

2

…will never have to face this beautiful sky.

1

I close my eyes as strong as I can, hearing the atrocious sound getting inexorably closer to me.

0

A dazzling white light approaches and invades me.

Isn't it ironic to die, seeing the purest light flourishing from the ashes of darkness?

Girin Orphée

Everything was silent. Just an anxious silence all around us. Everyone was looking at me, waiting for me to speak about him. I couldn't breathe anymore and all the pain of this tragic day came back to me.

I suddenly looked at my mom, who was crying, I looked at her and I said:

"Do you remember Steven's laughing when he thought he was alone? I wonder what he saw. What his world was like. Whatever he saw, it made him happy. I know it sounds silly to worry about a baby who looked too happy, but I felt that he had drifted away."

I lifted my head and I was petrified. What was wrong with me? I knew it was my entire fault. Maybe if I hadn't called that night… I had no right to be in front of them. But I continued:

"I know you did everything you could, Mommy. If only he could tell us about the world he saw. I don't think I would have understood, but I would have liked to try."

A lot more people were crying now. I saw it in their eyes: pity.

"There are so many things I don't understand... About Steven... About everything... But I know that everything that happened is not your fault and wherever Steve is now, I am sure he is happy."

The silence was now suffocating and everyone was holding their breath.

"And he wants you to be happy too."

MaévaPecqueux

October 31st

October 31st 1972. This date will remain forever engraved in my memory.

That night, which was a waking nightmare.
That night, during which I saw my whole life flash before my eyes.
That night, when I lost the only person I had on earth.
Today, I have decided to come out of the darkness in which I have been buried for 40 years, during which time I was unable to get a word out of my mouth or show any emotion.

My sister and I lost our parents during a car crash when we were only 7 years old. This was the first trauma of my life.

My twin sister was a journalist and was particularly interested in mysterious cases. She was endlessly on a quest for discovery. Namely, I have always supported her in what she was doing and have always been there for her. But that day I warned her not to go. I had a very bad feeling.

She wanted to interview a family with a reputation for being really weird and hiding secrets dating back centuries. I prevented her from doing so, but she only did as she pleased; I will eternally regret not having insisted more.

She asked me to accompany her to this manor, where the master had agreed to be interviewed.

I waited for hours -anxiety rising in me as if something bad was going to happen.- After the whole afternoon of waiting I decided to go and see what was going on -ignoring this feeling of dread in my stomach.

I knocked on the door, nobody answered.

So I tried to open it myself and then I couldn't contain my tears.

This was how she passed away.

S. M

Endless

Here I am. Again.

Walking without ever daring to stop. Walking as if I wanted to catch up with time, as if I were looking for time. *But why?*
It's a question that has been plaguing my mind ever since I woke up in the middle of this highway. Highway which overwhelmed me with a strange unbearable feeling of déjà-vu making my heart even heavier. Maybe it was because of the dozens of missing girl posters I had come across during this unfathomable walk. Or maybe it was because of this figure that kept following me.
Why wasn't my heart racing? Why was I devoid of any feeling of fear, devoid of any reaction? Why did this figure - which turned out to be that of a man - just walk past me as if I didn't exist?

"Come on Jane, get a grip. Stop psyching yourself out.", I reproached myself inwardly.

And that's when I saw it. A photo of a 16-year-old girl, surrounded by flowers and letters of condolence. "Rest in peace, Jane."

So this is where I got murdered.

Rihem M.

The "Foie Gras"

    This marvelous Foie Gras. How did it manage to get there, you may ask?
    Well, the story began when I met this tiny plump goose crawling in this deserted field near the local farmhouse.
    She was dirty and praying for Death to strike her the final blow.
    I was her savior, extending her life expectancy for years and treating her like my own child! …. If only.
    The reality is that I felt in her the enormous potential of being one of my finest meals of all time and could fast track my career into the most prestigious restaurants of Paris.
    I brought her back to my place and started cooking her. Right after I chopped her head, I immediately started

draining her blood from her body and removing this precious liver.

It was marvelous, her smell was extremely powerful and her texture extremely soft.

Obviously, I didn't have any sort of problems cooking her and after showing her to the most glamorous jury, they were completely shocked and I was instantly hired in a 4 Michelin star restaurant.

> So Dear little goose, even if I didn't change your life as you were expecting at least you changed mine.

VK

The Wood Reader

When I look… I feel. But when I observe… I understand. I was quite shocked when this little piece of art appeared in my sight. It looks as if it was entirely made of incomplex wood, whereas when I personally saw those fibers it became the storyline of the tree and more precisely, of the primary forest it comes from.

This tree appears in my mind as an untouchable hero who fought really hard with the devilish lumberjack but finally lost. He was the most powerful and respected in his forest. The one that newborn sticks wish they would become and the old branch would have loved to be in their youth. His death probably became a story of despair among the trees.

Primary forests are disappearing; in fact they lost 1.7 million hectares in 2020. We need to protect the trees and stop creating such useless items.

Now… He's a table… Constantly in a cycle of being half clean when people eat with disdain on him.

Please, educate your kids; they must care enough to be aware of what they despise.

So many stories are related to the object you see everyday. Please pay some respect as we know that every species is as evolved as we are, we're not better than the trees or the ants. Cancel

OUR POEMS

SURVIVOR TREE
New York city

Photo taken by V.K in 2022

This day when the alarm rung,

We didn't know what was awaiting us.

We jumped onto the fire truck,

We didn't have time to discuss.

Approaching New York, we saw huge plumes of smoke.

What happened to our Twin Towers, devoured by fire?

We were so shocked that none of us spoke,

Rescue the survivors was our only desire.

Ninetieth floor, I saw this young woman in panic coming down.

She was trying to put out the flames, I had to do it on my own.

Then with a shattering noise, the building collapsed.

So… Is it death? Perhaps.

There is nothing but darkness.

Lost in my fear and my prayers,

Am I still in the world and its curtness?

Suddenly, a ray of light, a ray of life, appeared through the layers.

We have to remember

For all these firefighters.

We have to hope

And not let go of the rope.

>DELLYS Quentin, JACQUET Julien,
>
>PHILIPPE Antoine, VOITURON Clément

Butterfly

On a cold fall day,
Flying between the building,
A colorful butterfly, thinking:
"What a beautiful Tuesday"

Finally has come the day
Suddenly, I became all gray
The towers crashed behind
This day, I will always remember

And in a few seconds, I turned colorblind
People were out of their mind
I saw the heaven door

From my ashes I reborn
Hope revealed my true color
"If I survive, all people can"

                                        PECQUEUX Maéva, PECQUEUX Yaël,
                                              GIRIN Orphée, LAUTH Martin

A glance of Hell

Psyches that I can't forget,
By those lines filled with regrets,
My tears are now writing this down
Since the attacks, missing is my own.

Everywhere stands fire,
Everywhere stands fear.

Surt I saw your anger hitting
I tried to stop your willing
My firehose, added to my bravery
Save souls: Remember Survivor tree.

In a blink I was sent in troubled water : Styx rivers,
Spite salt liquid in eyes, out at sea I saw my partners.

For the people that I couldn't save,
I'm still hearing your rales in my grave.
I felt I was a part of Thor's cells
Yet flames made me scared as in Niflhel.

I've fallen but you do not weigh, Chess Player ;
Even without rook, our knights will supplant her.

Dear thief of life, Dear robber of soul,
You'll not reach your goal, forsake idea of control.
There's still a seed of hope for those towers,
Like a glowing ember of a dying bonfire.

Saving your lives, my duty
Losing mine, for my country.

(Paragon of value before
Paragon of value after)

                        CANCEL Paul, CARPENTIER Axelle,
                        ENNEART Marie, KATSCHNIG Vitali.

GREETING CARD
BY MARIE ENNAERT
FOR JEAN BART HIGH SCHOOL

Acknowledgments

We, the A02 class, decided to create this piece of work in order to gather the products of our imagination in a book that would become a great souvenir of our year together as a group. It is also a way to contribute helping an association supporting the Ukrainian cause by the donation of our profits.

We would thus like to thank you, reader, for buying Mind Pastry, and showing an interest in our writing. We can't stress strongly enough how important we feel the help of our outstanding teacher, Ms Ghislaine Roussel and of Jacob our English assistant, was to us. Sincere thanks to Mister Valmalle too for allowing us to publish our work.

Furthermore, we also would like to thank Maéva Pecqueux for the fantabulous covers as well as Yaël Pecqueux and Orphée Girin for the gorgeous synopsis. A big thanks to Martin for the wonderful flyers too!

To finish, huge thanks and congratulations go to the participants of the project, the TG6 CLIL Senior Year, all of whom endeavored to create totally personal creative writings!

To all the trips we could have made!
Dunkerque, 05/19/2022